Emergency Medical Technicians

by Karen Bush Gibson

Consultant:
Dan Gerard, MS, RN, MICP
Chairman, National Paramedic Division
National Association of Emergency Medical Technicians

Bridgestone Books
an imprint of Capstone Press
Mankato, Minnesota

Bridgestone Books are published by Capstone Press
151 Good Counsel Drive, P.O. Box 669, Mankato, Minnesota 56002
http://www.capstone-press.com

Library of Congress Cataloging-in-Publication Data
Gibson, Karen Bush.
    Emergency medical technicians/by Karen Bush Gibson.
    p. cm.—(Community helpers)
    Includes bibliographical references and index
    Summary: A simple introduction to the clothing, tools, schooling, and work
of emergency medical technicians.
    ISBN 0-7368-0623-7
    1. Emergency medicine—Juvenile literature. 2. Emergency medical
technicians—juvenile literature. [1. Emergency medical technicians. 2. Occupations.]
I. Title. II. Community helpers (Mankato, Minn.)
RC86.5 .G52 2001
610.69'53—dc21   00-026921

Editorial Credits
Sarah L. Schuette, editor; Timothy Halldin, cover designer; Katy Kudela,
    photo researcher

Photo Credits
David A. Boer/South Dakota Emergency Medical Services for Children, 4, 10
Index Stock Imagery, 16
International Stock/Charlie Westerman, 12; Dario Perla, 18
Jack Glisson, 6
James L. Shaffer, 8
Leslie O'Shaughnessy, cover, 14, 20

1 2 3 4 5 6 06 05 04 03 02 01

Table of Contents

Emergency Medical Technicians

Emergency medical technicians give medical care to people during an emergency. People call these workers EMTs. EMTs also drive ambulances that take people to hospitals quickly.

emergency
a sudden and dangerous situation

What EMTs Do

EMTs help people who are hurt. They often work together in teams of two or more people. EMTs may travel to the scene of a car crash or a fire. They travel anywhere that people need medical help. EMTs treat people's injuries and take people to the hospital.

injury
damage or harm
to the body

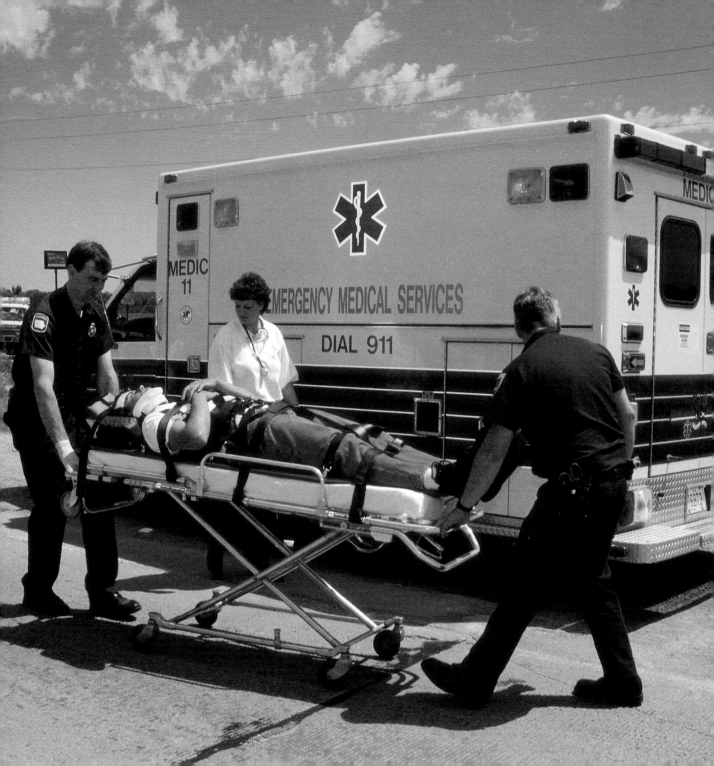

What EMTs Drive

EMTs must know how to drive an ambulance. Ambulances move quickly. Sirens and flashing lights warn people to move out of the way. EMTs use radios and phones inside the ambulance to talk to doctors and nurses at hospitals. Some EMTs fly in helicopters.

siren
an object that makes
a loud noise

Tools EMTs Use

EMTs use life-saving tools. They use masks to give oxygen to people who cannot breathe. They put bandages on cuts. EMTs put splints on broken bones. They use backboards to carry people who are hurt.

oxygen

a colorless gas in the air; people breathe oxygen to stay alive.

Where EMTs Work

EMTs work in police departments, hospitals, and fire departments. They need to be ready at all times to help in an emergency. Some EMTs are volunteers. Volunteers do not get paid for their work.

What EMTs Wear

EMTs wear clean and neat uniforms. They also wear clothes for all types of weather. EMTs sometimes have to wear sterile gloves. Gloves help EMTs stay safe and healthy.

sterile
free of germs

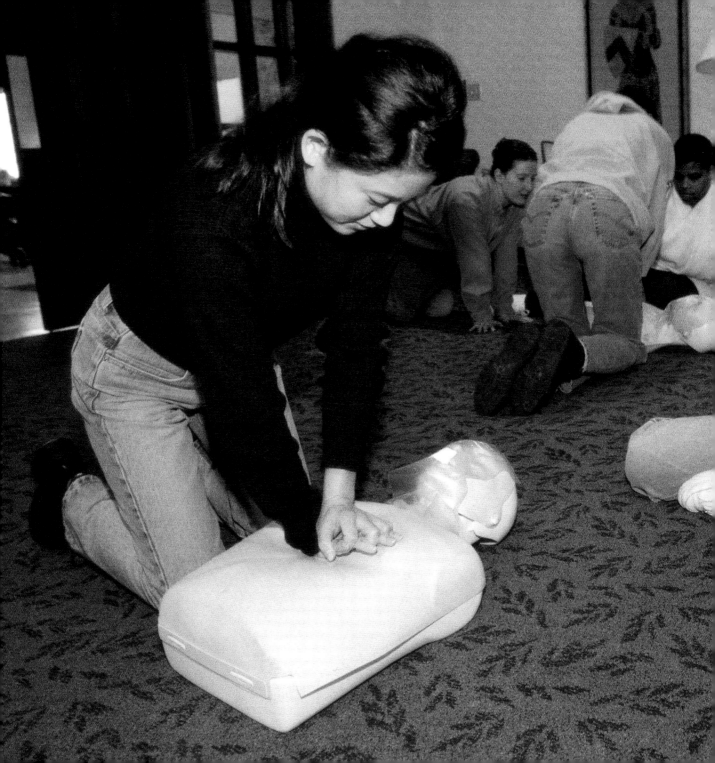

EMTs and School

EMTs take classes to learn how to take care of sick and injured people. They learn first aid. EMTs practice their skills in classrooms and hospitals. They also take classes to learn how to drive ambulances or to fly helicopters.

first aid
emergency care given
to injured or sick people

People Who Help EMTs

Dispatchers help EMTs by answering emergency calls. They then call EMTs when someone needs medical help. Dispatchers tell EMTs the best route to drive. Doctors and nurses also help EMTs. They take care of the people EMTs bring to hospitals.

dispatcher
a person who gives messages and directions

19

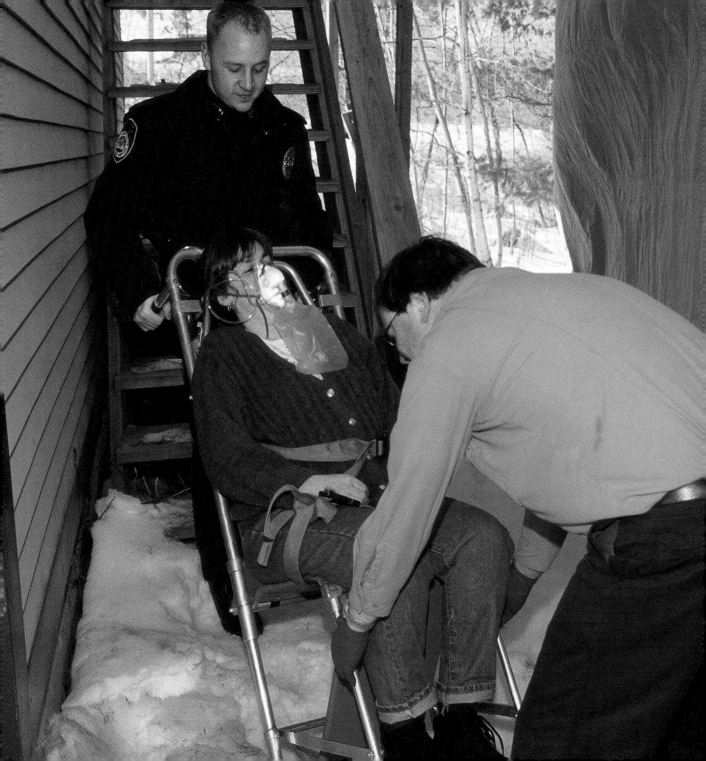

How EMTs Help Others

EMTs sometimes are the first people to help during an emergency. EMTs work together to treat people's injuries quickly and safely. EMTs save lives.

Hands On: Breathing Test

EMTs check to make sure people are breathing after an emergency. They are trained to breathe air into a person who is not breathing. EMTs need strong lungs. You can test the amount of air your lungs hold.

What You Need

An empty 1-gallon (3.8-liter) plastic milk jug with a cap
Pen
Dish pan
Water
3 feet (91 centimeters) of small plastic tubing
Ruler

What You Do

1. Make a mark near the top of the plastic jug with the pen. Fill the jug with water up to the line. Fill the dish pan with water.
2. Put the cap on the jug and turn it upside down in the dishpan. Take the cap off. Keep the mouth of the jug underwater.
3. Place one end of the tubing into the mouth of the jug. Do not let air into the jug.
4. Take a deep breath and blow into the other end of the tube. Use the ruler to measure how much water goes out of the jug in one breath. Refill the jug with water and repeat.

Words to Know

backboard (BAK-bord)—a large board used to carry people who are hurt and cannot walk

helicopter (HEL-uh-kop-tur)—an aircraft that can take off and land in a small space

oxygen (OK-suh-juhn)—a colorless gas in the air; people breathe oxygen to stay alive.

route (ROUT)—the road or course people follow to get from one place to another

splint (SPLINT)—a piece of wood, plastic, or metal used to support an injury

volunteer (vol-uhn-TEER)—someone who does a job without getting paid

Read More

Bowman-Kruhm, Mary and Claudine G. Wirths. *A Day in the Life of an Emergency Medical Technician.* Kids' Career Library. New York: Rosen, 1997.

Freeman, Marcia S. *Ambulances.* Community Vehicles. Mankato, Minn.: Pebble Books, 1999.

Royston, Angela. *Emergency Rescue.* Des Plaines, Ill.: Heinemann Interactive Library, 1998.

Internet Sites

911 Kids Playhouse
http://home.worldnet.att.net/~v.defrance/911kids.htm
Safety City EMS Department
http://www.nhtsa.dot.gov/kids/ems/index.html
Toronto Ambulance-Just for Kids
http://www.city.toronto.on.ca/ems/kids/just_for_kids.htm

Index